The Vegetarian Pesach Cookbook

Feasts for Freedom

Roberta Kalechofsky

Cover art work by Sara Feldman

Production by Robert Kalechofsky and Roberta Kalechofsky

Acknowledgements: Ilustrations: Carol Belanger Grafton, *Victorian Floral Illustrations*, Dover Pictorial Archive Series, 1985; Jim Harter, *Food and Drink*, Dover Pictorial Archive Series, 3rd edition, 1983; Hal Aqua and Risa Towbin Aqua, The Big Book of Jewish Borders, Headers and Fillers, A.R.E. Publishing, 1994.

ISBN: 978-0-916288-47-1

Micah Publications, Inc.
www. micahbooks.com

TABLE OF CONTENTS

We bless You, Lord, Our God,
Creator of the Universe
Who creates the vegetables from the ground

We Bless you Lord, our God,
Creator of the Universe,
Who creates the fruit of the tree

The Vegetarian Pesach Cookbook
Feasts for Freedom

Introduction

What's In A Name?

For generations, The Festival of Matzoh has been called Passover or Pesach, but that is not what Moses called it, or the Hebrews of that first generation who went out into the desert with him to worship the God Who had called them out of Egypt. They named the occasion "The Festival of Matzoh."

> Remember this day on which you went free from Egypt, the house of bondage, how the Lord freed you from it with a mighty Hand: no leavened bread shall be eaten. You go free on this day, in the month of Nisan. So, when the Lord has brought you into the land of the Canaanites, the Hittites, the Amorites, the Hivites, and the Jebusites, which the Lord swore to your fathers to give you, a land flowing with milk and honey, you shall observe in this month the following practice:
>
> Seven days you shall eat unleavened bread, and on the seventh day there shall be a festival of the Lord. Throughout the seven days unleavened bread shall be eaten; no leavened bread shall be found with you, and no leaven shall be found in all your territory. And you shall explain this to your child on that day, 'It is because of what the Lord did for me when I went free from Egypt.' (Ex.13:3-8)

From its inception, Pesach was regarded as the Festival of Unleavened Bread, or Hag ha Matzoh, and unleavened bread was the symbol of both poverty and freedom.

Oded Schwartz writes that the original meaning for Pesach was not a reference to the 'passing over' of the angel of death on the night the Hebrews prepared to leave Egypt, but to the "leaping, skipping or gamboling of newborn ewes and lambs." Pesach was a spring celebration of renewal and birth. The Festival of Unleavened Bread begins on the night of the full moon of the vernal

The environmentalist case against a meat-centered diet is beyond argument now. "The feed cost of an eight ounce steak will fill 45 to 50 bowls with cooked cereal grains." Christopher Flavin, president of Worldwatch Institute, stated that "There is no question that the choice to become a vegetarian or lower meat consumption is one of the most positive lifestyle changes a person could make in terms of producing one's personal impact on the environment." The impact on the environment affects every aspect of global human life, our medical bills, famines and poor nutrition in Third World countries, our national economy, our poor eating habits. According to Eric Schlosser's book, *Fast Food Nation*, "Americans now spend more money on fast food--$110 billion dollars a year--than they do on higher education. They spend more on fast food than on movies, books, magazines, newspapers, videos and recorded music--combined." This formidable meat steamroller affects the availability of energy.

Energy and power are continually lost in our food supply: It takes 78 calories of fossil fuel to get 1 calorie of protein from beef, and 2 calories of fossil fuel to get 1 calorie of protein from soybeans. The United States leads the world in the production of soybeans, but feeds most of it to animals.

One struggle for freedom in this generation is to throw off our bondage to foreign sources of energy. The strategy for this is to change from a meat-centered diet to plant based nutrition. It is not the total solution, but it is an important part of the solution, and it is importantly that part of the solution that each one of us can be responsible for.

Cattle today dominate the earth. They take up one fourth of the land mass of the planet. Worldwatch Institute estimates that there are 20 billion head of livestock on the earth, more than triple the number of people, and that the global livestock population has increased 60 percent in the last forty years, the number of fowl raised for food has nearly quadrupled from 4.2 billion to 25.7 billion; U.S. beef and pork consumption has tripled in the last forty years and doubled in Asia. According to a *Time* magazine article (1999), livestock in the United States produces 130 times more waste than people do. "There are more chickens processed annually in the United States than there are people in the world--7.6 billion chickens versus 6 billion humans." (Robbins, *The Food Revolution*). There are 300 million turkeys in the United States compared to 280 million Americans, and a 100 million hogs and 60 million head of cattle. The effect of all this on the health of the earth and on our personal health is staggering. Quoting from *Newsweek*, *E Magazine* wrote, "...the factory-farmed chicken, cow or pig of today is among the most medicated creatures on Earth. For sheer over-prescription, no doctor can touch the American farmer." The waste from such numbers is even more staggering; the fecal build-up in waterways and on agricultural land that is buried under manure soaked with chemicals is responsible for the spread of new forms of food poisoning, including our fruit, vegetables and grain. To use the analogy of secondary smoke, the secondary effects of meat agriculture are felt everywhere.

The Vegetarian Pesach Cookbook
Feasts for Freedom

Introduction

What's In A Name?

For generations, The Festival of Matzoh has been called Passover or Pesach, but that is not what Moses called it, or the Hebrews of that first generation who went out into the desert with him to worship the God Who had called them out of Egypt. They named the occasion "The Festival of Matzoh."

> Remember this day on which you went free from Egypt, the house of bondage, how the Lord freed you from it with a mighty Hand: no leavened bread shall be eaten. You go free on this day, in the month of Nisan. So, when the Lord has brought you into the land of the Canaanites, the Hittites, the Amorites, the Hivites, and the Jebusites, which the Lord swore to your fathers to give you, a land flowing with milk and honey, you shall observe in this month the following practice:
>
> Seven days you shall eat unleavened bread, and on the seventh day there shall be a festival of the Lord. Throughout the seven days unleavened bread shall be eaten; no leavened bread shall be found with you, and no leaven shall be found in all your territory. And you shall explain this to your child on that day, 'It is because of what the Lord did for me when I went free from Egypt.' (Ex.13:3-8)

From its inception, Pesach was regarded as the Festival of Unleavened Bread, or Hag ha Matzoh, and unleavened bread was the symbol of both poverty and freedom.

Oded Schwartz writes that the original meaning for Pesach was not a reference to the 'passing over' of the angel of death on the night the Hebrews prepared to leave Egypt, but to the "leaping, skipping or gamboling of newborn ewes and lambs." Pesach was a spring celebration of renewal and birth. The Festival of Unleavened Bread begins on the night of the full moon of the vernal equinox. Many seders incorporate references to the joyousness of the spring season by including passages from the Song Songs. Solomon Zeitlin, in volume three of his history, *The Rise and Fall of the Judean State*, points out that the term, Passover, has a religious meaning in the context of animal sacrifice, while the name, Festival of Matzoh, has a national meaning; it refers to the birth of a nation and symbolizes political independence and nationhood. He observes that the name, Pesach, is not biblical and that it came to be used after the fall of Judea. It is the name which is familiar to us, but we should keep in mind its references to spring, birth, and renewal, not to sacrifice.

The history and symbolism of unleavened bread predates the Hebrew nation. It was the common bread of nomadic tribes in the Middle East, and defined the nomad as much as potatoes defined the lower classes in the West in recent times. According to John Cooper the word "matzoh" derives from the Assyrian "massartu." In old Babylonia, ma-as-sa-ar-tu always meant barley, which was the principal cereal used to make bread in the ancient world. The Greek word for barley is "moza." The Egyptians are credited with having discovered the properties of yeast and were considered masters of the art of baking. But because risen bread takes time and special conditions to bake properly, risen bread became associated with the settled or city life, which the nomad scorned. Tradition states that the reason the Hebrews took unleavened bread with them is because it was practical to do so. The more profound meaning is that they took unleavened bread with them because it symbolized their condition of servitude and their political aspirations. The symbolism of unleavened bread is unquestionable: it was the bread of poor people, of a servant class, of nomads.

We today have a reverence for the Temple--or what remains of it, which is the wall Herod built--because of two millennia of being deprived of our Jewish political center. In the absence of political autonomy, the Temple wall became a powerful symbol of a lost homeland. But our nostalgia should not be confused with what Jews felt for the Temple when the Temple actually stood and functioned. Since the days of the prophets, particularly since Isaiah, the Temple had been a target of criticism and condemnation for centuries. By the year O CE, most Jews lived in the diaspora throughout the Roman world, in Greece, in Alexandria and in Rome, and the Temple did not function in their daily lives except as a symbol of the political center of Jewry. It did not function as a source of purification, of penitence, or as a way of ratifying the meat they ate. Jews everywhere paid their yearly half shekel tax for the maintenance of the Temple, as we pay our taxes today, but the Temple scarcely functioned in their lives except if they made a pilgrimage to Jerusalem, which afforded them the opportunity to eat meat if they chose to, for there is no commandment in the Bible to eat meat. The commandment is that if you do eat meat, you must sacrifice your animal properly. For Jews in the diaspora, there was no legitimate Temple in which to do this.

Without a Temple, diaspora Jews developed formats and rituals which became standard for them and for the rest of Jewry after the fall of the Temple. The synagogue and the home were the loci of Judaism in the diaspora and became increasingly so for all Jews after the fall of the Temple. The home was already enshrined in Torah as the place for the transmission of Jewish values, learning, history, and religion. In Deut. 6:4-5, the home is singled out as the significant institution of Jewish life:

> Hear O Israel: the Lord our God, the Lord is One. And you shall love the Lord your God with all your heart, and with all your soul, and with all your might. And these words which I command you this day shall be upon your heart. You shall teach them diligently to your children and shall speak of them when you sit in your house, and when you walk by the way, and when you lie down, and when you rise up.

Again in Deut. 6:20:

> You shall teach My words to your children, talking of them when you sit in your house

For those in Judea, there is evidence that the Temple was regarded with tense ambivalence. The idea of the demise of the Temple had been "in the air" for decades. In his book, *The Origins of the Seder*, Baruch Bokser suggests that the rabbis knew that the sacrificial cult was coming to an end as an institution and were preparing to substitute other symbols for the loss of the pascal lamb in the seder.

> Aquiva implies that the loss of the paschal rite, after the temple's destruction, should not produce any extraordinary concern, for its loss forms part of the general loss of the sacrificial cult....the end of the paschal sacrifice is not a unique catastrophe.

Formats were developing both within Judea and the diaspora to convey penitence, purity and repentance, without sacrifice, so that when the Temple lay in ruins, and a disciple asked Rabbi ben Zakkai, "What will we do now that the Temple is gone?" ben Zakkai did not say that we will rebuild; no such thought apparently crossed his mind. What he said was, "We will now have prayer and deeds of loving kindness," and set out to preserve Judaism in a new form at Javna. The fall of the Temple made rabbinic Jewry possible.

The association of meat with holiday celebrations was declared no longer to be in effect after the sacrifices ended. A Talmudic text states: "In the days when the Temple was in existence, there was no rejoicing without meat...but now that there is no longer the Temple, there is no rejoicing without wine...." (Rabbi

Judah ben Betairah, *Beit Yoseph*). Jews are commanded to celebrate the holidays with wine and with joy, but there is no halachic requirement to celebrate them with meat. Baruch Bokser has called the transference from the Temple to the home a "cultic transference," which brought with it ritualistic changes. The importance of sacrifice was de-emphasized to emphasize the vitality of the Jewish religion which could--and did--transcend the loss of the Temple and the sacrificial system. The seder table played a part in the "cultic transference." The emphasis on sacrifice was diminished and the status of charoset, matzoh and bitter herbs was elevated We know from statements in the Talmud that there were Jews who refused to place a shankbone on the table, because the Talmud provides for its substitution with a beet or a mushroom. We suggest grapes, olives and unfermented grain (kept in saran wrap to keep from fermenting) because of the statement in Deut. 24:20, which commands us to leave the second shaking of the vine tree for the poor, and the second shaking of the olive tree for the poor, and that neither should we muzzle the ox when he treads out the grain in the fields. We call these mitzvoth of compassion for oppressed creatures. Other people have suggested making a shankbone out of papier maché so that we can commemorate the lamb which was sacrificed on the night of deliverance.

After the fall of the Temple, the focus of Jewish celebration shifted from the Temple to the synagogue and the home, and the table in the home came to be regarded as an altar, where every Jew can officiate over the commandments for holiness. Rabbi Moshe Isserlis (16th century Poland) declared, "The table is like an altar and the meal is an offering." (*Hilcot B'tziyat Hapat*, 167:5)

Modern Bondage

The Bible has fixed the image of slavery in our minds,but there are many forms of bondage and slavery. For most of the world, poverty is the seedbed of slavery. Working in sweatshops for enough money to purchase one meal a day is surely a form of slavery if one can never rise out of that condition. Parents sell their children into slavery for money to feed the rest of their family; workers sell themselves into slavery for passage money to a free world. Jews themselves have been enslaved in more ways than the Bible speaks of. During the European Middle Ages, their legal status was that of "servants of the treasury." Jews were legally required to make money for Christians through usury, as they once were forced to make bricks in Egypt. European medieval documents are replete with references of barons and kings giving Jews as a gift or as a dowry, or used as barter in exchanges. Jews were slaves in Nazi camps during the Holocaust. Each era seems to bring its own kind of slavery, not only for Jews but to other peoples. The Anti-Slavery Society publishes newsletters with classifications of slavery, from child sex prostitutes to "house servants" in Third World countries who are not free to leave their masters, to sweat shop workers who are not free to leave their sweat shops, to agricultural workers who cannot leave the land they are "bonded" to. This information can be accessed on their United States website, www.iabolish.com

There are parallels and emphases in history between the Exodus 4,000 years ago and our enslavement today to fossil fuels and oil. In our time in the West, the danger is that we will march into our own form of slavery through the wide doors of prosperity. Torah tells us that the Hebrews lived in luxury at first and did not wish to see their coming enslavement until it was too late for them to escape it. Robert Kaplan, author of *The Coming Anarchy*, and others warn that the coming struggle in the twenty-first century will be over resources, as our water sources dwindle and as much of our earth turns to desert.

A few short weeks before September 11th, 2001, vice-president Dick Cheney was asked at a conference why the government does not advocate conservation to solve our energy problem. His answer was memorable and deadly. "Conservation is all right as a personal morality, but it can't make a national policy." It was the personal morality of hundreds of firefighters, police, ambulance drivers, nurses, doctors, and others who came to Ground Zero in New York to help, that brought us through the intolerable experience when the Twin Trade Towers were destroyed. How much more awful it would have been without the personal morality of those who reached out to help. It is the personal morality and heroism of soldiers that Dick Cheney and President Bush depend upon to fight our wars. Conservation must be a national policy if we are to reclaim our national independence and not be enslaved to foreign powers. Conservation is politically and morally right. Furthermore, conservation must be implemented sooner or later because the oil reserves will run out sooner or later, not in some mythical time of centuries from now, but possibly within the lifetime of our children and grandchildren. An article in *The Economist* (Nov.3-9, 2001), "Sunset for the Oil Business?" debates the subject. The question is not whether the oil will run out, but whether it will run out in a matter of decades or generations, and how much the price of oil will rise as it starts to run out.

Changing our meat-centered diets could release sources of energy that are now being used to run megalithic factory farms, and such change would make land available that could be used to generate alternative sources of energy. Suggestions for "windmill farms" are not fantastical but practical, if we release the land for this use. In *The Food Revolution*, John Robbins writes:

> If we ate less meat, the vast majority of the public lands in the western United States could be put to more valuable--and environmentally sustainable--use. Much of the western United States is sunny and windy, and could be used for large-scale solar energy and wind-power facilities. With the cattle off the land, photovoltaic modules and windmills could generate enormous amounts of energy without polluting or causing environmental damage. Other areas could grow grasses that could be harvested as 'biomass' fuels, providing a far less polluting source of energy than fossil fuels.

The environmentalist case against a meat-centered diet is beyond argument now. "The feed cost of an eight ounce steak will fill 45 to 50 bowls with cooked cereal grains." Christopher Flavin, president of Worldwatch Institute, stated that "There is no question that the choice to become a vegetarian or lower meat consumption is one of the most positive lifestyle changes a person could make in terms of producing one's personal impact on the environment." The impact on the environment affects every aspect of global human life, our medical bills, famines and poor nutrition in Third World countries, our national economy, our poor eating habits. According to Eric Schlosser's book, *Fast Food Nation*, "Americans now spend more money on fast food--$110 billion dollars a year--than they do on higher education. They spend more on fast food than on movies, books, magazines, newspapers, videos and recorded music--combined." This formidable meat steamroller affects the availability of energy.

Energy and power are continually lost in our food supply: It takes 78 calories of fossil fuel to get 1 calorie of protein from beef, and 2 calories of fossil fuel to get 1 calorie of protein from soybeans. The United States leads the world in the production of soybeans, but feeds most of it to animals.

One struggle for freedom in this generation is to throw off our bondage to foreign sources of energy. The strategy for this is to change from a meat-centered diet to plant based nutrition. It is not the total solution, but it is an important part of the solution, and it is importantly that part of the solution that each one of us can be responsible for.

Cattle today dominate the earth. They take up one fourth of the land mass of the planet. Worldwatch Institute estimates that there are 20 billion head of livestock on the earth, more than triple the number of people, and that the global livestock population has increased 60 percent in the last forty years, the number of fowl raised for food has nearly quadrupled from 4.2 billion to 25.7 billion; U.S. beef and pork consumption has tripled in the last forty years and doubled in Asia. According to a *Time* magazine article (1999), livestock in the United States produces 130 times more waste than people do. "There are more chickens processed annually in the United States than there are people in the world--7.6 billion chickens versus 6 billion humans." (Robbins, *The Food Revolution*). There are 300 million turkeys in the United States compared to 280 million Americans, and a 100 million hogs and 60 million head of cattle. The effect of all this on the health of the earth and on our personal health is staggering. Quoting from *Newsweek*, *E Magazine* wrote, "...the factory-farmed chicken, cow or pig of today is among the most medicated creatures on Earth. For sheer over-prescription, no doctor can touch the American farmer." The waste from such numbers is even more staggering; the fecal build-up in waterways and on agricultural land that is buried under manure soaked with chemicals is responsible for the spread of new forms of food poisoning, including our fruit, vegetables and grain. To use the analogy of secondary smoke, the secondary effects of meat agriculture are felt everywhere.

Inevitably, meat production takes its toll on available energy. Meat diets take a disproportionate toll on our energy supply, and consequently on our dependence on foreign sources of oil. Meat plays a significant role in our enslavement to foreign powers. According to *E Magazine* (Jan-Feb., 2002), "Producing a single hamburger patty uses enough fuel to drive twenty miles and causes the loss of five times its weight in topsoil." As John Robbins wrote in *Diet For A New America,*

> The social, ecological and economic consequences as we...turn away from animal food products, are equally remarkable....The water crisis ceases. As we stop raising and grinding up cattle for hamburgers, we discover that ranching and farm factories have been the major drain on our water resources. The amount now available for irrigation and hydroelectric power doubles...As expenditures for food and medical care drop, personal savings rise--and with them the supply of lendable funds. This lowers the interest rate, as does also the drop in oil imports which eases the pressure on the national debt.

The Union for Concerned Scientists, in a 1999 report, stated that the two worst contributors to environmental degradation are the automobile and animal agriculture. Survival in the modern world of the future requires a sane public transportation system and a food system that is not meat-centered. Individually, we have only indirect control over the implementation of a public transportation system, but everyone of us has control over our animal agricultural system by not eating meat. Diet is not only a question of personal morality, it is a question of national survival. Animal agriculture and meat production in the United States use more energy per capita than the less developed countries spend per capita on energy for all combined purposes. Animal agriculture uses over 90% of the agricultural land in the United States, or over half of the total land area of this country; it uses hundreds of billions of gallons of water everyday for crop irrigation that is fed to animals; animal agriculture is a major contributor to deforestation in the United States, in Central and South America. Animal agriculture destroys topsoil and pollutes waters and rivers with tons of contaminated fecal runoff from cows. The sum total of all this waste is the omnipresent threat of famine in underdeveloped countries where monocultures and animal agriculture are encouraged by the United States. These farming policies lead to devastation in Third World countries, which in turn lead to jealousy, bitterness and hatred. A memoir from the World Food Summit held in Rome, November, 2001 described an "economic imperialism imposed on developing countries by meat conglomerates."

> Several US meat companies are growing into transnational conglomerates by acquiring domestic and foreign firms and by pushing policies

> and trade agreements that would vastly expand their production capacity and markets in developing countries. Most of this expansion would involve massive, cruel 'factory farming' operations that would eventually breed, raise, and slaughter as many as 100 billion animals per year in the world. Such operations would also devastate the local food supplies, environmental resources, public health, and economic infrastructures.... The meat industry is directly responsible for 85 percent of all soil erosion in the U.S., because so much grain is needed to feed animals being raised for food. In the U.S., animals are fed more than 80 percent of the corn we grow and more than 95 percent of the oats. Raising animals for food is grossly inefficient, because you have to put 20 calories of food into an animal to get just one measly calorie back in the form of 'flesh.' The world's cattle alone consume a quantity of food equal to the caloric needs of 8.7 billion people--more than the entire human population on Earth.

Quoting from The Worldwatch Institute, the memo continued, "Roughly 2 of every 5 tons of grain produced in the world are fed to livestock, poultry, or fish; decreasing consumption of these products, especially of beef, could free up massive quantities of grain and reduce pressure on the land." A diet that feeds valuable foods such as soybeans, corn, and grain to animals, and then eats the animals who eat the soybeans, corn, and grain is the stupid house that stupid Jack builds.

In 1998, the Worldwatch Institute, warned that

> We have altered vast ecosystems and devoted massive resources to support our livestock populations, which have grown much more rapidly than human population since mid-century. The ecological footprint of world meat production includes forest destruction for ranching in Central and South America, suppression of native predators and competitors in the United States, and the introduction of invasive forage species virtually everywhere commercial ranching exists....The massive quantities of waste produced by livestock and poultry threaten rivers, lakes and other waterways. In the United States, where the waste generated by livestock is 130 times that produced by humans, livestock wastes are implicated in waterway pollution, toxic algae blooms and massive fish-kills....According to EPA, the world's livestock herds account for roughly 25 percent of anthropogenic emissions of methane --a potent greenhouse gas contributing to climate change. Moreover, as the stagnant waste lagoons of factory-farmed operations emit an additional 5 percent of human-induced methane, making livestock production the largest source of anthropogenic methane emissions.

When the first astronauts returned from outer space what they reported changed the way we view the earth. Looking back upon planet earth from outer space, the astronauts were awestruck by the interconnectedness and fragility of everything on the planet. Some have compared this new view of planet earth to the revolutionary conception Copernicus wrought when he disproved that the earth was the center of the universe. Rivers, streams, ponds, oceans, bays, all waterways, rain, clouds, fog, the mist that falls, everything that is moist, that holds water, that releases water, is related. If you contaminate streams and lakes in Georgia, the contamination will make its way around the world. If you have a nuclear accident in a remote city in Russia, the radiation fallout will find its way to Lapland. Wind and water carry our devious designs against nature, our poisons, the sick excrement of sick animals, bacteria, viruses, flues, epidemics. Poisonous vapors rise from the earth and cast a veil over what once would have been the healing power of the sun.

We cannot unlearn or ignore what we now know: that everything on the earth is interconnected. If we destroy the rainforests to make land available for meat, we will alter the climate of the earth; if we allow the unchecked growth of food animals, we will destroy our waterways, our soil and our climate. The world is round and everything is interconnected, and nothing dictates that the earth can withstand every assault. Interconnectedness and fragility characterize the home we have been given. There is an old adage which should haunt us: "God always forgives, humans forgive sometimes, nature never forgives." A new meaning for Passover should be "pass over the meat."

Tamarisk Trees and Manna

A root in the story of Exodus stretches back to Abraham's journey through the Negev where he planted tamarisk trees. The tamarisk is a desert tree, the leading tree in all deserts because of its root system. It is very hardy and can survive under difficult conditions, though it bears dainty pink and white flowers. The city of Beer-Sheva has adopted the tamarisk tree as its emblem because it guards the town against sandstorms that blow there. More importantly, the tamarisk tree is the source of the manna which the Hebrews ate in the desert.

The Bible is specific in its description of manna: (Numbers 11:7).

> Manna was like a coriander seed, bdellium in color. The people would gather it, grind it between millstones, pound it in a mortar or boil it in a pot and make it into cakes. It tasted like rich cream.

Claudia Roden, in *The Book of Jewish Food*, tells us that Jews still eat a sweet food called "manna from heaven" (p. 23), and her description of it resembles the manna described in the Bible. It is a cake

cruelty, and many carry the potential dangers of salmonella and campylobacter food poisoning. For many communities it is possible to find eggs from local farms where healthy chickens still run free, scratch in the soil, and drink in the sun. If you are lucky enough to be able to buy your eggs from such a farmer, encourage him to stay with the old fashioned way of raising chickens. It may cost a bit more, but good farming practice is invaluable in the long run. You might make a visit to an independent farm part of your Pesach celebration. Then the connection with spring and fertility would have more meaning.

Instead of an egg on the seder table which came from a sick chicken, replace the egg with flowers, or with an egg made from papier maché, and explain to your children what the substitution means.

Kitnyot

In November, 1997 Rabbi David Golinkin, representing the Rabbinical Assemby of Israel--Vaad Halacha--issued an important response to the question as to whether it is permissible to eat legumes and rice during Pesach. One of the questions posed to Rabbi Golinkin was: "In the light of the ingathering of the exiles, would it be possible to eliminate the Ashkenazi custom of not eating legumes on Pesach?"

Rabbi Golinkin's response was an unequivocal "yes." The full text is in Hebrew, but the English version states that it is not only permitted to eat legumes and rice but it is perhaps even obligatory "to eliminate this custom," because it is a divisive custom between Sephardic and Ashkenazic Jews, because it diminishes the joy of the holiday, and because it has little authoritative sanction. Rabbi Golinkin wrote: "In our opinion it is permitted (and perhaps even obligatory) to eliminate this custom. It is in direct contradiction to an explicit decision in the Babylonian Talmud (Pesahim 114b) and is also in contradiction to the opinion of all the sages of the Mishna and Talmud, except one...."

The custom of not eating legumes and rice began in the thirteenth century in France and Provence, but "the reason for the custom is unknown and as a result many sages invented at least eleven different explanations for the custom." Rabbi Golinkin pointed out that most rabbinic authorities opposed the custom. Rabbi Samuel of Falaise "referred to it as a 'mistaken custom,'" and Rabbi Yeruham called it a "foolish custom."

Rabbi Golinkin addressed the halachic question as to "whether it is permissible to do away with the mistaken or foolish custom." Again, his response was an unequivocal "yes." "Many rabbinic authorities have ruled that it is permitted (and perhaps even obligatory) to do away with this type of 'foolish custom'..."

Rabbi Golinkin also pointed out that by adhering to the custom of not eating legumes, it places an undue emphasis on this custom and tends to diminish the importance of the chametz. Indeed, in Torah, when the holiday is first pronounced by Moses, the forbidden food is simply unleavened bread.

This decision has special significance for Jewish vegetarians who eat no animal products and whose sources of protein are limited during this holiday, but it is an important decision for all Jews because it increases the joys of the appetite and of eating from a table that represents the bounty of a bountiful Creator. This cookbook takes advantage of the new guidelines, but if you feel uncomfortable eating legumes and rice, omit the recipes that have these ingredients, or consult your rabbi.

If you use the recipes which include kitnyot, then use organic, fresh beans or rice. Do not use canned beans, which have been processed and may not be kosher for Pesach. It is easy enough to soak a package of fresh beans and cook them.

What Shall We Eat?

Pesach—the Festival of Freedom-- is an excellent time to renew--or to become acquainted for the first time--with the world of organic food, with non-processed food, with fruits and vegetables, and to explore the numerous recipes that can be made with non-meat ingredients. Everything is ripening and reaching our supermarkets. Among our staples are potatoes, eggplant, cauliflower, broccoli, onions, nuts, greens, avocados, parsnips, tomatoes, leeks, carrots, cucumbers, cabbage, kale, squash, sweet potatoes, beets, parsnips. From these we can make dozens of dishes.

Cholesterol and animal products are not our only concerns in these recipes. There are many enemies in American food, particularly in processed foods. We selected dishes that did not require salt, or much salt or sugar. You're free to add these according to your taste. If you use salt, use a sodium-free salt, and if you use sugar, use organic sugar.Where recipes call for matzoh farfel, you can make your own by grinding matzohs in a food processor. Add herbs to matzoh farfel for an interesting topping or base to vegetable and nut loafs. Use your own taste and common sense with any recipe---and any cookbook.

Nuts and Nut Roasts:

One of the most popular vegetarian dishes for the main course on the first night of Pesach is the nut roast. In several cases, matzoh farfel was substituted for breadcrumbs. While there may be concern about the fat content of nuts, nuts are too healthy to avoid and their fat content is of the treasured unsaturated kind, which helps to lower "low-density-lipoprotein (L.D.L.) cholesterol." This is not true of walnuts, but walnuts are a good source of omega 3. An article in *The New York Times* (Feb. 8, 2000) by Jane Brody stated the importance of nuts in our diet (except if you are allergic to them):

> Nuts contain several vitamins and minerals that protect against heart diseases, high blood pressure and stroke, including folate, which lowers blood levels of homocystein. Elevated levels of homocystein can triple the risk of heart attacks. Peanuts are the best source of folate, followed by hazelnuts and walnuts....Beneficial minerals in nuts include calcium, magnesium and potassium, and all protect against high blood pressure. Pistachios followed by almonds are the richest nut sources of potassium, and almonds are the best nut source of calcium. Brazil nuts are rich in selenium, which may prevent prostate cancer....

For this reason it is good to use mixed nuts in your nut roasts.

All this may be true, you say, but nuts have a dark reputation for being fattening, and even if "I get fat on the good sources of fat, fat is fat." In the same article Jane Brody pointed out that "when nuts and nut products are included in a calorie-controlled diet, they may actually improve dieting success." It's not the nuts that lead to fat, it's the nibbling. A study at the Brigham and Women's Hospital in Boston showed that women who ate 35 percent of calories from fat whose source was "nuts, peanuts, olives and olive oil," stuck to their diets over the long haul and lost more weight than women whose diets included only 20 percent calories in fat because they went off their diets and gained back their weight.

Nuts also make an inestimable contribution to the Pesach table because one can make nut crusts for pies.

Searching for Chametz

Pesach begins the night before the first seder--sometimes two and three nights before, when the house is cleaned of all leaven products, down to the last crumb. This is a good time to clean the house of meat products and processed foods. It is a good time to take the pledge for a healthier diet.

The Table As An Altar: Setting The Table

In *The Vegetarian Epicure* (Book Two) Anna Thomas wrote: "A good menu is like a good story. It must have the proper balance of dramatic elements, sorted out and arranged in such an order that each new course fulfills the promise of the one that came before, while setting the scene for the one to follow, and everything must be resolved in the end, for unlike some stories, all meals should have endings."

What is a better story than the redemption from slavery and the creation of the Jewish people? What story has a better ending? Our table and our food should reflect the seriousness and the joy of this story.

The Matzoh is the central symbol on the table, usually enshrined on a beautiful matzoh plate, covered with a matzoh cloth.

The other ritual foods are greens for dipping in salty water. Greens can be celery or parsley, whatever is convenient; bitter herbs, which is usually a dish of horseradish; charoset, and a shankbone in the form of papier maché or a substitute for the shankbone, such as olives, grapes and unleavened grains. Some families have special seder plates, but this is not necessary. You can make any tray look beautiful with these foods and with flowers.

Cups with salty water strategically placed so that everyone can dip their greens
Cups of wine for everyone and a cup of wine for Elijah
Candles, yarmulkas and haggadahs

Charoset

Charoset has captured the Jewish culinary imagination, perhaps because its ingredients have lovely associations, as the following passage from the *Shulkhan Aruch* testifies and demonstrates how highly symbolic Jewish food can be:

> "It is proper to prepare the charoset out of fruits to which the people of Israel are likened--for instance, figs, because it is written:

The fig-tree perfumeth its green figs (Song of Songs, 2:13); nuts, because it is said 'into the nut-garden I had gone down (Song of Songs, 6:1); 'dates because it is said, "I wish to climb up the palm-tree' (Song of Songs 7:9), pomegranates, because it is said, 'Like half the pomegranate' (Song of Songs 6:7). Apples, in commemoration of what is said: 'Under the apple tree have I waked thee' (Song of Songs, 8:5)...and almonds, because the Holy One, blessed be He, was anxious to bring about their redemption.

Jewish communities around the world have created numerous recipes for charoset. There is a tradition for charoset which is made from every fruit mentioned in the Song of Songs. Sephardic charoset often includes figs, dates, and raisins rather than apples. Claudia Roden in *The Book of Jewish Food* includes a recipe for charoset from Italy, which is made with apples, pears, pine nuts, almonds, and dates. Joan Nathan in her book, *The Jewish Holiday Kitchen*, has a recipe for charoset from Venice, which includes chestnut paste, poppy seeds, pine nuts, dried apricots, brandy and honey. She also has an intriguing recipe from Surinam, that is made with unsweetened coconut, walnuts and almonds, raisins, dried apples, dried prunes, dried apricots, dried pears, cherry jam and wine. Because one of my daughters-in-law is allergic to fresh fruit and nuts, but not to cooked fruits and nuts, I make the traditional recipe, but boil the fruits and nuts for about ten minutes, long enough to render the allergic properties in these ingredients null. I discovered that boiling walnuts and apples, then mixing them in the food processor, adding wine and cinnamon, made a delicious paste. Obviously, one's imagination can run rampant devising new, enticing charoset dishes. What all the charoset dishes have in common is that they remind us of the mortar used by Jews when we were slaves in Egypt and of the sweetness of liberty.

Charoset

The following is a standard recipe .

3 apples peeled, cut in large chunks
1/3 cup chopped walnuts or almonds
1/4 teaspoon cinnamon
1-2 tablespoons kiddush wine

In food processor fitted with steel blade, combine apples and nuts and process until finely ground. Scrape into a bowl and add cinnamon and sugar to taste. Add enough wine to make a paste, or whatever consistency you prefer. Make the charoset a few days in advance to let the flavors ripen. Serves 8-12 as is, but double the amount and you will be able to enjoy the leftovers for dessert or snacks on matzoh rounds.

MAIN DISHES

The contemporary pattern to dispersion in the West today is often the result of mobility, and our pilgrimage is usually to the home of parents or grandparents or the matriarch or patriarch of our families. Families live apart. The holidays bring them back together, if only temporarily.

"In Jewish families, cooking has always revolved around the Sabbath and religious festivals....The dishes chosen to celebrate these occasions became part of festive rituals and acquired embellishments as they acquired symbolic significance. They were glamorized to glorify the occasions....

Dishes are important because they are a link with the past, a celebration of roots, a symbol of continuity. They are that part of an immigrant culture which survives the longest....

'We will be near to becoming one nation when we can sit at each other's tables without feeling unease or strangeness. Liking each other's foods is a big step towards liking each other.'"

Claudia Roden, *The Book of Jewish Food*

No food is more divisive than meat.

Vegetable Nut Loaf 1

This dish was adapted from Rose Friedman's *Jewish Vegetarian Cooking*. It can be made earlier in the day and popped into the oven in late afternoon. The trick to this loaf is to baste it and keep it moist. Nut loafs, lentil loafs and vegetable loafs are good to serve with oven roasted potatoes, because you can pop them into your oven and roast together.

Oil for baking pan
1 large onion, finely chopped
3 cloves of garlic, finely chopped
2 large carrots, grated
3 cups of mixed ground nuts
1 cup matzoh meal
4 tablespoons tomato paste
1 large onion, sliced thinly
2-1/2 cups vegetable stock

Preheat oven to 350 F.
Mix all ingredients, except vegetable stock and sliced onion.

Oil ovenproof dish approximately 9 X 12; place sliced onions over the bottom.

Form nut and carrot mixture into a loaf and place on top of sliced onions.
Bake 45 minutes.
Baste with vegetable stock every 20 minutes. Remove from oven and let cool for ten minutes.
Serves 8.

Tip: Ingredients can be cut in half for a smaller loaf, but don't worry about having too much: tastes good the next day if left at room temperature. If you make a smaller loaf, use a smaller loaf pan.

Vegetable Nut Roast11

This is adapted from Freya Dinshah's recipe in her book, *The Vegan Kitchen,* published by The American Vegan Society. Simple to make, does not require much cooking in the oven, since the ingredients are already cooked, but does require some pre-preparation for vegetables.

oil for oven dish
2/3 cups Brazil nuts
2/3 cups filberts
2 medium potatoes, peeled
2 small zucchini squash
1 medium sweet potato (or small butternut squash)
1 large carrot
4 ribs celery
1 small onion, peeled
2-2/3 cups matzoh meal
1-1/2 teaspoons mixed herbs
4 teaspoons olive oil
2 tablespoons of paprika

Preheat oven to 350 F.
Cover nuts with water and simmer until soft (about one hour).
Drain, dry, and grind.
Dice all the vegetables and cook together in about 3-1/2 cups of water for about 30 minutes. Drain and mash. Mix in the nuts
Add the matzoh meal, oil and herbs. Mix well.
Put mixture into a small oiled baking pan, press down well. Sprinkle paprika on top.
Pop into oven for about ten minutes to give the roast a nice browning.
Serves 4-6

Variations: You may want to put a mushroom sauce over this loaf, or serve with cooked mushrooms and/or caramelized onions. It depends on how ambitious you are and how much time you have during this week.

Lima Bean Roast

This roast is also adapted from Freya Dinshah's book, *The Vegan Kitchen,* and requires some preparation the night before to cook the lima beans. It is an unusual combination of ingredients, but note that this recipe is only for 4-5 and should be made when you're not expecting a crowd.

oil for loaf pan
2/3 cup dry lima beans
water
1 large onion, finely diced
1-1/2 teaspoons potato flour
1-1/2 tablespoons of unsalted roasted peanut butter
1 cup of matzoh farfel
1/2 teaspoon of mixed herbs, thyme, basil, etc.
2 sliced tomatoes
salt to taste

Soak lima beans overnight in 3 cups of water
Drain lima beans
Cook lima beans and diced onion in 3 cups of fresh water for about 1 hour and 20 minutes

Preheat oven to 400 F
Mash lima beans with potato masher
Mix in potato flour and peanut butter, herbs and matzoh farfel.
Oil a small loaf pan, approximately 5 X 9
Put in ingredients in alternating layers: 1/2 bean mixture; sliced tomatoes, 1/2 bean mixture.
Bake 30 minutes
Serves 4-5

Tip: If you cannot get kosher for Pesach peanut butter, buy a package of unsalted peanuts and grind in a food processor to the consistency of peanut butter. Also, if loaf feels a bit dry, add a little oil to it before baking.

Vegetable Bake

Adapted from a Pesach classic from *Jewish Vegetarian Cooking* by Rose Friedman

8 ounces fresh spinach
2 medium onions, chopped fine
1 small green pepper, de-seeded and diced
1 clove garlic, crushed
olive oil for frying
1 rib celery, chopped
3-4 medium carrots, grated
salt and pepper, to taste
pinch of ginger
1 tablespoon tomato purée
1/2 cup ground mixed nuts
1/4 cup matzoh meal
1/3 cup vegetable stock

Preheat oven 350 F.
Wash spinach well, cook and chop finely.
Sauté onions green pepper and garlic until soft
Add celery and carrots, cook for about 10 minutes, stir frequently
Mix all the vegetables together. Add seasonings, tomato purée, nuts, and matzoh meal. Mix well.
Place in oiled ovenproof loaf pan, approximately 5 X 9
Pour the hot stock over the loaf. Bake for about 30 minutes or until brown on top, or an inserted toothpick comes out clean.
Serves 6

Variation: sprinkle sweet paprika on top for a nice brown look, or hot paprika for a spicier taste, but sprinkle hot paprika sparingly.

Stuffed Cabbage With Squash

We often think that cabbage should be stuffed with chop meat, but you can stuff cabbage with anything. Here is one suggestion that is succulent.

Preparation: Bake butternut squash
Boil water in a very large pot

One large head of green cabbage, washed
4-5 cups of mashed butternut squash
Oil for a large rectangular baking dish
1 large cup of walnuts, chopped
2 teaspoons of nutmeg
pinch of salt

Sauce:
one 16 ounce cans of tomato sauce
3 tablespoons mild vinegar, or to taste
1-1/2 tablespoons ground cinnamon
1 cup raisins (optional)

Preheat oven to 350 F
While squash is baking, boil water in a very large pot
Put whole head of cabbage into boiling water and boil for about twenty minutes or until outer leaves of cabbage look limp
Drain the cabbage and let cool .
When squash is soft, remove from oven, cut in half, clean out seeds and pulp, and mash the squash
Add chopped walnuts and cinnamon to squash

When cabbage is cool enough to handle, gently pull away large outer leaves, place a large tablespoon of squash in each leaf, roll up, pin sides together, and place on large oiled baking dish, 9 X 12.
Mix ingredients for sauce and pour over the stuffed cabbage. Add 1/2 cup raisins, if desired. Bake 20 minutes. Remove and cover baking dish with aluminum foil to prevent the sauce from drying out.
Serves ten

Tip: Make sauerkraut from left over cooked cabbage. Shred and marinate in equal parts of mixture of good vinegar and water. Add sliced green peppers, if desired.

Festive Sweet and Sour Cauliflower Bake

A dish that looks beautiful and tastes like it looks:

1 tablespoon oil
1 medium onion
1 large head cauliflower
3 medium sweet potatoes
3 McIntosh apples

Sauce:

1 8 ounce can tomato sauce
2 tablespoons tomato paste
1 tablespoon plus 1 teaspoon balsamic vinegar
2 tablespoons cinnamon

Preheat oven to 375 F
Oil a large baking dish (9 X 12)
Slice onions and layer bottom of dish
Wash cauliflower, break into small flowerlets and place on top of onions
Wash and cut potatoes and apples into chunks, place on top of cauliflower

Blend all ingredients for sauce and pour over the dish. Make sure to coat the vegetables and the fruit
Bake 1 hour, in oiled baking dish, covered.
Serves 6

Variation: Add 1 cup apricots or one cup diced dates. If you have a sweet tooth, add both.

Tip: To increase serving, add one more sweet potato and one more apple, and oil a larger baking dish. If you eat rice, this is a good dish to serve over rice. If served over rice, will serve 8-9 without adding extra potato and apple.

Mushroom, Eggplant Moussaka

Adapted from Mollie Katzen's Mushroom Mousaka in *The Moosewood Cookbook.* Mollie Katzen is one of the great pioneers in the vegetarian movement. Many of her recipes, such as the following, convert well to a vegan diet.

Preheat oven to 350 F.

One large eggplant or two medium eggplants
2 pounds mushrooms
1 large onion, chopped
2 tablespoons olive oil
2 cloves minced garlic
1/4 cup chopped parsley
1/2 teaspoon salt
1/2 teaspoon cinnamon
6 ounces tomato paste
dash of oregano and basil
1/4 cup red wine
3/4 cup matzoh farfel

Slice eggplants 1/2 inch thick, bake on oiled cookie sheet 15 minutes, or until just tender

Clean and slice mushrooms, sauté in oil with onion and garlic
Add parsley, tomato paste, oregano, basil, salt, cinnamon, and wine.
Simmer until liquid is absorbed.
Add 1/2 cup matzoh farfel

Oil a round casserole dish. Cover bottom of the dish with eggplant slices. Pllace half the mushrooms over the eggplant slices, the rest of the eggplant slices, end with mushrooms. Top with 1/4 cup matzoh farfel. Bake 35 minutes covered; 5 minutes uncovered to brown the matzoh farfel.
Serves 8

Tip: Use a 1/4 cup herbed matzoh farfel on top of casserole (see recipe, p. 59)

Vegetable and Matzoh Casserole

This takes a bit of time because each ingredient has to be cooked separately, but it can be prepared earlier in the day and popped into the oven 20 minutes before serving.

3 tablespoons olive oil
1 large onion, sliced thin
2 cloves garlic, minced
1 medium-large eggplant, peeled and cubed
1 green pepper, diced
1 red pepper diced
3/4 pounds mushrooms, washed and sliced
2 large tomatoes, cut into small chunks
1 can tomato sauce
2 cups herbed matzoh farfel (see recipe, p. 59)

Preheat oven 350 F
Sauté onion in oil, add garlic. Remove onion and garlic and drain on paper towel
Sauté eggplant, remove eggplant from skillet and drain on paper towel
Sauté green and red pepper together, remove from skillet
Sauté mushroom
Sauté tomatoes

Layer oiled round casserole dish with matzoh farfel, vegetables, herbed matzoh farfel, ending with herbed matzoh farfel. Top with tomato sauce.
Bake 20 minutes
Serves 8

Variation: Plain matzoh farfel instead of herbed matzoh farfel if you don't like the herb taste

Multi-National Potato Casserole

The original version of this dish is Kurdi-Iraqi, and it was made in individual deep-fried portions. We adapted it for a lower-cholesterol dish.

2 tablespoons oil
4 cups sliced mushrooms (about 1 pound)
2 cups chopped onions
1/2 cup slivered almonds
1/2 cup golden raisins
Salt and pepper
8 medium red skin potatoes, boiled and peeled
2 teaspoons ground cumin
1/2 teaspoon ground turmeric
1-3 tablespoons warm water, stock,
or reserved potato cooking water
2 tablespoons margarine, melted

Heat 2 tablespoons oil in 10 " or 12" skillet. Sauté onions and mushrooms until onions are tender and mushrooms give up their liquid. (You may need to cover the skillet for part of the cooking time, especially if you are using a 10" skillet.) Add raisins, almonds, and a sprinkling of salt.

Preheat oven to 375 F.
Oil an 8 cup casserole, about 7" x 11", or 8" x 8".

Mash potatoes. If necessary, add 1 tablespoon or more of warm liquid to make potatoes workable. Season with cumin, turmeric, salt and pepper, and add most of the melted margarine.

Place a layer of mashed potatoes in the bottom of casserole. Cover it with mushroom mixture. Top with the rest of the potatoes, and brush with remaining margarine. Bake for about 40 minutes.
Serves 8.

Variation: If you wish to eliminate cumin, flavor potatoes with a small chopped onion sautéed in melted margarine or oil. Use turmeric for its golden color.

Roasted Veggie Pizza

The next three recipes are recommended for a chol-hamoed dish. The first recipe is time-consuming, but worth it when you're looking for an unusual Pesach dinner. The recipe was adapted by Mimi Golfman-Clark from *Eating Well.*

2 cloves garlic, minced
3 cups thinly sliced red onion
1/2 cup water
1/4 cup balsamic vinegar
1 tablespoon maple syrup
1 teaspoon thyme, divided
1/2 teaspoon sea salt
1 red bell pepper, roasted and cut into thin strips
1 yellow bell pepper, roasted*
and cut into thin strips
4 fresh basil leaves, slivered
1/2 teaspoon dried rosemary
1/2 teaspoon dried oregano
matzoh meal to sprinkle on peel, stone or pan
Prepared potato pizza base: see below

Preheat pizza baking stone (if using) in 500 F oven.

In a large saucepan, place garlic, onions, water, vinegar, maple syrup, 1/2 teaspoon thyme and salt.
Cook, covered on low heat, stirring frequently 45-60 minutes until liquid evaporates and onions are slightly caramelized; cool. (This mixture can be made in advance and refrigerated.)
Distribute onion mixture over baked potato crust. Scatter peppers over onions.
Sprinkle rosemary, oregano and 1/2 teaspoon thyme on top.
Bake 10-15 minutes.
Serves 6

*To roast peppers: wash and dry peppers. Place on a cookie sheet about 4" under the heat of a broiler. (You can use a stovetop grill or gas burner, but these can be messy) Char the peppers on all sides until the skins blacken.

Transfer peppers to a paper bag or covered bowl; close bag allowing peppers to steam for 15 minutes. Rub off charred skin under cool water; seed, derib, and cut into strips. Can be done ahead. *(continued)*

Potato Crust Base For Pizza

(From *Jewish Vegetarian Cooking*, by Rose Friedman)

1 1/4 pounds potatoes, boiled or steamed, and cooled
1 tablespoon margarine
3/4 – 1 cup matzoh meal
1/4 cup potato flour
1/2 teaspoon sea salt

Mash potatoes, add margarine. Mix in matzoh meal, potato flour and salt. Knead by hand until dough forms a ball. If dough is too stiff, add a few drops of water; if dough is too 'pasty,' gradually add more matzoh meal.

Wrap dough in plastic wrap and refrigerate at least one hour. (Dough may be made the day before and refrigerated. If so, leave at room temperature to soften a bit before using.)

Lightly spray 2 pans, 7" X 11" or one 12" pizza pan. Roll dough to fit pans. Bake 20 minutes, until crusty and browned. Top with vegetables

Fasta-Than-Pasta -Tomato Farfel Bake

You can put this dish together in 5 minutes. It comes out of the oven tasting like pasta with a light tomato sauce. Reheated, it tastes like scalloped tomatoes.

2 1/2 cups crushed, peeled, unsalted, canned tomatoes
1/4 cup chopped onion
1/2 teaspoon salt
1/4 teaspoon pepper
1 tablespoon sugar
1 1/2 cups matzoh farfel
1/4 cup oil

Preheat oven to 375 F.
In a medium bowl, combine tomatoes, onion, salt, pepper and sugar.
In another bowl, mix farfel and oil.
Oil a 1 quart baking dish. Put a layer of the farfel mixture in the bottom of the dish, then a layer of tomatoes.
Repeat, ending with farfel.
Bake 30 minutes or until lightly browned.
Serves 6

Chili With Vegetables

We eliminated the soy granules from the original recipe created by Gloria Bakst, featured in *The Jewish Vegetarian Year Cookbook*

1 large onion, chopped (about 3/4 cup)
2 cloves garlic, crushed
1/4 cup dry vermouth or white wine
2 tablespoons chili powder
1/4 teaspoon dried basil
1/4 teaspoon dried oregano
1/4 teaspoon cumin
2 cups finely chopped zucchini
1 cup finely chopped carrot
1 29 ounce can tomatoes plus 1 14 1/2 ounce can tomatoes, drained and chopped
4 cups cooked kidney beans + one cup of their cooking water
1 tablespoon brown sugar

<u>Garnish</u>

Chopped onions, tomatoes, lettuce and green pepper

In a 4 quart or larger pot, sauté onion and garlic in wine until soft. Mix in chili powder, basil, oregano and cumin. Stir in zucchini and carrots. Cook for about 1 minute over low heat, stirring occasionally. Add chopped tomatoes, kidney beans with the 1 cup cooking water, and brown sugar. Stir well. Bring to a boil, reduce heat, and simmer for 30-45 minutes or until thick. Top with vegetable garnish.
Serves 8-10.

Variation: Can be served over rice.

Tip: Best if prepared in advance to let the flavors set in. Leftovers can be reheated or served cold.

Soups

Soups are wonderful to serve for this holiday because they can be made in advance. In fact, many soups, like stews, benefit if they stand for twenty-four hours, so this is one dish you don't have to cook on the same day you will be serving.

It's easy to vary the taste of traditional soups by adding different herbs like dill, curry, thyme, and even nutmeg. These herbs can take the place of salt, or allow you to reduce the amount of salt you use.

You can also add an exotic flavor to some soups like tomato soup, by adding 1/4-1/2 cup of wine or sherry. We'll leave the amount up to you.

You can purée soups in a food processor, but a blender is a handy kitchen tool. It allows you to purée the soup in the pot, without having to go to the fuss of transferring the soup from soup pot to food processor, and back to soup pot.

It is also handy to have vegetable stock on hand. Some cooks prepare their stock in advance, freeze them into cubes and use the cubes as needed. A substitute for this are vegetarian bouillon cubes, which will add flavor. However, you may not be able to find kosher for Pesach bouillon cubes, so it may be best to make your own soup stock. How much water and/or stock you use depends on how thin or thick you want the soup to be.

Vegetable Stock

This vegetable stock recipe is an unusual one, and can also be used as a tomato-vegetable soup.

2 Spanish onions, chopped
2 leeks, white and green parts, chopped
2 large carrots, cut in chunks
2 celery ribs, cut in chunks
28 ounce can crushed Italian tomatoes, or the equivalent made from fresh tomatoes
10 large parsley sprigs
10 thyme sprigs or 1 teaspoon dried thyme
2 teaspoons whole black peppercorns
4 quarts water

Combine all ingredients in a large stock pot. Bring to a boil; adjust heat and simmer uncovered about 1-1/2 hours. Skim foam from stock as necessary. Drain through a fine sieve. Press vegetables down firmly with the back of a spoon to extract all the juices and flavors. Discard solids or save for later use. Makes 3 quarts.

Tip: If not using stock immediately, freeze in containers of various sizes, 1 cup, I pint, I quart, as you anticipate use in the future.

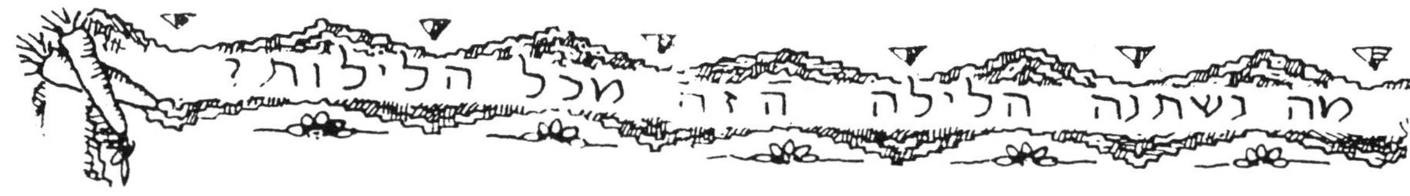

Broccoli Soup

It's easy to make common soups exotic by adding an interesting spice or herb. We do this in the next two recipes.

1-1/2 tablespoons olive oil
one large onion, chopped
two ribs of celery, chopped
one large head of broccoli.
6 cups of water
2 vegetarian bouillon cubes
1/4 cup minced parsley
1/2 teaspooon nutmeg

Break broccoli into flowerlets. Reserve stalks for later use in broth.
Heat oil in a large pot
Sauté onion about 5 minutes. Add chopped celery, sauté another five minutes
Add broccoli, water, bouillon cubes and parsley.
Cover pot and cook for 30 minutes. Purée.
Add nutmeg and stir.
Serves 6-8

Tip: If you want to make the soup "creamy" add a small mashed potato. The thickness of the soup is optional. If you prefer a thinner soup, use more water.

Variation: Sprinkle roasted matzoh farfel on the soup or place dishes with them on the table and let your guests do the sprinkling.

Cauliflower Soup

2 tablespoons of olive oil
one large onion, diced
1 large head of cauliflower, broken into flowerets
1 large carrot, grated
6 cups water
2 vegetarian bouillon cubes
2 tablespoons dill

Heat olive oil in large soup pot
Sauté onion briefly, about five minutes
Add cauliflower, carrot, water and bouillon cubes.
Cover pot and cook for thirty minutes. Purée.
Sprinkle dill on top and cook for another two minutes.
Serves 8

Variations: This soup lends itself to many variations.
Instead of dill, use 1 tablespoon of curry.

Omit curry and sprinkle 2 tablespoons of grated carrots over each bowlful. Adds color as well as flavor. Or squeeze half a lemon for a zestful taste.

Omit curry. Add 2 cups of washed spinach ten minutes before cooking is done. This color combination is also beautiful.

Add 1-1/2 cups cooked chickpeas.

Tip: If you want to make the soup "creamy" add a small mashed potato. The thickness of the soup is optional. If you prefer a thinner soup, use more water or stock.

Golden Glow Soup

This is a soup I recommend for Shabbat. Those who feel comfortable eating legumes can make it for Pesach.

1 pound package (2 cups dry) yellow split peas
1 cup grated parsnips
1 cup grated carrots
Salt to taste
3 bay leaves

Cook yellow split peas according to directions on package.
Halfway through cooking time, add parsnips, carrots, salt and bay leaves. Simmer with partially covered lid. Remove bay leaves before serving.
For a golden color and smoother taste, purée.
Serves 8.

This soup goes well with eggless matza balls .

Eggless Matzoh Balls

4 medium potatoes
1-1/4 cups (approximately) matzoh meal
pepper to taste
Water or vegetable broth

Peel, dice and boil potatoes until soft. Mash potatoes, add peppper to taste. Add matzoh meal gradually. Knead until firm and smooth. Form small smooth balls.
Fill a large soup pot 3/4 full with water or broth and boil. Drop matzoh balls into boiling water, cover pot, cook for about 20 minutes. Do not overcook. Serve with soup.

Tip: Refrigerate matzoh balls for a few hours before cooking. You can now buy commercial vegan matzoh balls in some speciality shops.

Leek and Potato Soup

2 large leeks, trimmed and cleaned, white parts only
1 pound Yukon gold potatoes, peeled, cut in 1/4" dice
2 tablespoons margarine
1 cup finely chopped onions
3 cups vegetable stock
2 cups water
1 bay leaf
Salt and freshly ground pepper to taste
Minced fresh chives

Chop leeks in 1/4" lengths. Melt margarine in 3 quart or larger saucepan. Add onions and leeks. Cook over medium heat until golden and limp. Add potatoes, stock, water, bay leaf, salt and pepper. Bring to simmer and cook for 30 minutes, or until potatoes are tender.

Discard bay leaf. Use a potato masher to partly mash potatoes; if you prefer a thicker, smoother soup, put soup in processor fitted with steel blade and pulse until desired thickness. Correct seasonings. Garnish with chives. Serves 4-6.

Tip: You can use other varieties of potato, but the Yukon Gold gives the soup a rich golden color. If you want the soup to keep its golden color, serve the same day.

The plant foods the Israelites in the desert longed for were garlic, onions, leek, melon and cucumber. Cultivation of the leek is very ancient. There is evidence of it as far back as 2100 BCE in Ur. Its cultivation in Egypt is as old as Egypt's history. The Greek historian, Herodotus, wrote that leeks were among the food rations fed to the slaves in Egypt.

Curried Green Pea Soup

A simple soup to make which makes an exotic impression

1 pound package (2 cups dry) split green peas
1 medium onion, chopped
1/2 cup chopped celery
1 teaspoon salt, or to taste
2 teaspoons curry powder, or to taste

Cook according to directions on green pea package. When soup is done, add curry. Cool, then purée in blender or with hand held device.
Goes well with matzoh farfel.
Serves 6-8.

Tip: If Pesach falls out on a warm spring night, serve this soup chilled.

Velvety Green Pea Soup

1 tablespoon vegetable oil
1 1/2 cups chopped onions
2 teaspoons crushed garlic
2 carrots, peeled and chopped
1/2 pound mushrooms, sliced
6 cups vegetable stock
2 medium potatoes, peeled and diced
2 (20 ounce) bags frozen sweet peas (about 6 cups) divided
1-1/2 teaspoons dried rosemary
1-1/2 teaspoons dried thyme
Salt to taste

In a 4 quart non-stick saucepan, heat oil. Sauté onions, mushrooms and carrots until just tender, about 5 minutes. Add garlic and sauté one minute more.

Add stock, potatoes, and all but 1/2 cup of the peas.
Simmer, covered, for 20-25 minutes, or until potatoes are tender, adjusting heat as necessary.

In food processor, or with blender, purée soup until perfectly smooth.
Reheat, add herbs and remaining peas.
Serves 8.

Tip: Can be made early in the day and refrigerated until ready to serve. Reheat gently.

Butternut Squash Bisque

A great flavorful soup if Pesach falls out on a chilly March evening.

2 teaspoons unsalted margarine
2 large carrots, peeled and sliced
1 cup chopped onion
1 clove garlic, minced
1 tablespoon minced fresh ginger
2 teaspoons curry powder
1/4 teaspoon ground cinnamon
1/8 teaspoon ground nutmeg
2 medium butternut squash,
about 2 pounds each, peeled, seeded and cut into chunks
3 cups apple juice

Melt margarine in a 3 quart saucepan over medium heat.
Add carrots, onion and garlic.
Cook over medium-high heat until tender, about 5 minutes.
Add ginger, curry, cinnamon and nutmeg. Cook for 1 minute.
Add squash and apple juice.
Heat to a boil.
Cover, reduce heat and simmer for 15 minutes or until squash is tender.

Purée soup in several batches in blender or processor until smooth. Reheat.
May be served hot or chilled.
Serves 6-8.

Tip: This soup thickens, so if a thinner soup is desired, add water a little at a time, to reach desired consistency.

Salads, Vegetables & Side Dishes

Vegetables are the most companionable of foods. You can mix most any vegetables together and create a wonderful cooked vegetable dish or salad. The variety is almost infinite. Choose the freshest vegetables, buy organic if you can. You rarely have to do anything to good vegetables, except perhaps a brief sautéeing or steaming if you want them cooked. Try sautéeing some vegetables, like cauliflower, in roasted sesame oil for a different taste sensation.

For salads, we usually use only olive oil and vinegar for dressing, but you may want to choose some other dressing. We give salads variety through herbs, particularly basil or dill. A little finely diced onion and a pinch of garlic powder can add spice. You can also try different kinds of vinegars to vary taste sensations. Use rice vinegar for a milder vinegar taste.

Potatoes are the most commonly used vegetable in Pesach meals. They're easy to cook in a variety of ways, and are a good starch for those days when you can't fill up on carbohydates through bread, rice, or pasta. They're not suggested, however, for people who have serious diabetes.

Oven-Roasted Potatoes

A quick, easy, but tasty recipe when you are using the oven

1 medium size potato per person
3 tablespoons olive oil
Tarragon, oregano, rosemary
or paprika to cover potatoes lightly
Salt to taste

Preheat oven to 400^0 F.
Oil a cookie tin liberally (but not too liberally).
Cut potatoes into large cubes, salt lightly, sprinkle with spice or herb, to taste.

Bake for about 1 hour, turn once or twice to make sure potatoes brown evenly.

Variation: Halfway through cooking time, add zucchini, cut into 2" chunks. The combination of potatoes and zucchini is attractive and delicious. You can also add red peppers, or a combination of red and yellow peppers for a very colorful dish.

Baked Potatoes

If you think a baked potato is too ordinary you can make them worthy of a holiday dish by scrubbing, cleaning, drying with paper toweling, then rolling in olive oil before baking.

Variations: Roll in herbed olive oil: Mix oil with basil or the herb of your choice.

Turn baked potatoes into potato boats. Use potatoes with nice long shapes. Cut in half after baking, scoop out potatoes and mash with margarine or oil, diced scallions and parsley, salt and pepper to taste. Fill potato skins with mixture, sprinkle paprika on top of each potato half, return to oven for 5 minutes to brown

Potato and Garlic Casserole

Another easy potato dish for the seder. This can be made early in the day and kept at room temperature until 10 minutes before serving. Reheat uncovered, in oven at 350^0 F.

2 small red potatoes per person, scrubbed, left whole
1 garlic clove for every two potatoes
1/4 cup olive oil
Salt and pepper to taste
Paprika
Tarragon or rosemary to taste

Preheat oven to 350^0 F.
Place potatoes in oven casserole just big enough to hold them in a single layer. Roll in oil to cover. Spread whole garlic cloves between potatoes. Sprinkle salt, pepper and spices to taste. Pour olive oil on top. Cover and bake 50 minutes to 1 hour. Pop in the oven uncovered 10 minutes before serving.

The potato is one of the world's most important foods. The United Nations Food and Agricultural Organization has called it "The world's fourth largest food crop after corn, wheat and rice." Frances Moore Lappé and Joseph Collins in *Food First,* wrote that "It is one of only fifteen food products which feed the entire world." In 1912, Georges Gibault wrote that the potato "is the most useful gift which the New World has made to us."

Baked Diced Potatoes

8 cups peeled, diced potatoes
(about 6 medium large)
4 tablespoons oil
1/3 cup minced onion
1 cup minced celery
1/4 cup minced parsley
1 1/2 teaspoons salt
1/4 teaspoon freshly ground black pepper

Place potatoes in 3 quart pot. Cover with cold water; bring to boil. Reduce heat and simmer 5 minutes; drain.

Preheat oven to 375° F.
Mix potatoes with remaining ingredients.
Oil a large, shallow baking dish and put potatoes in it. Bake 30 minutes or until the potatoes are golden and just beginning to brown.
Serves 8

Potato-Mushroom Kugel

A rich, hearty kugel. It can be prepared in advance and reheated in oven 15 minutes before serving.

2 tablespoons oil
6 medium size potatoes,
peeled, and diced for cooking
2 tablespoons of margarine
1 large onion diced
1/2 pound mushrooms
3 large portobello mushroom caps
salt and pepper to taste

Preheat oven 400 F.
Cook potatoes until soft and mash with margarine with a masher. Do not mash in a food processor because this changes the consistency of the potatoes.
Clean, and remove stems from portobello mushrooms and roast in oven for 20 minutes. Remove caps and slice into strips.
Sauté onion in oiled skillet
Add mushrooms to onions after onions have begun to brown slightly. Drain remaining liquid from skillet.
Add mushroom and onion mixture to mashed potatoes, salt and pepper to taste.
Turn into an oiled 9 X 12 casserole
Decorate top with portobello mushroom strips
Turn oven down to 350F. Bake for 10-15 minutes
Serves 8-10

Variation:For a richer taste, marinate portobello mushrooms for 1/2 hour in 2 tablespoons tomato paste, 1/4 cup wine, 1/2 cup water, 1/4 cup oil, 1 teaspoon garlic powder.

Tip: For weight-conscious guests, use liquid from mushroom-onion mixture instead of margarine in the mashed potatoes.

Sauté portobello mushroom stems with onion-mushroom mixture for richer taste.

Knishes

A great recipe if you are having many guests for your seder. The recipe looks long but it's really simple and you can make the components a day or two ahead--or make the complete recipe and freeze.

Potato Dough Knishes

3 large baking potatoes, peeled and quartered (enough for dough and filling)
1 tablespoon or more potato cooking water, or stock

Other Dough Ingredients:

3 tablespoons margarine
3 tablespoons vegetable shortening
3/4 cup potato starch
1/2 teaspoon salt
Dash pepper

In medium saucepan, bring to boil potatoes and water to cover. Reduce heat, cover, and simmer until potatoes are tender, about 15 minutes. Drain well, return to pan, and shake gently over low heat to dry.

Mash potatoes in the pan with a fork or masher, adding seasonings and enough liquid to hold them together. Measure one cup of mashed potatoes for dough and reserve remainder for filling.

To make the dough: In a small mixing bowl cut shortening and margarine into flour with pastry blender or two knives. When well combined, add measured cup of mashed potatoes and mix well. Form the dough into a ball, wrap in plastic wrap, and chill at least 20 minutes. May be kept overnight.
Makes enough pastry for about 2 dozen small knishes.

(Continued)

Potato-Onion Filling

1 1/2 to 2 cups mashed potatoes
1 to 1 1/2 cups chopped onions
1 tablespoon oil
Salt and freshly ground black pepper

Heat oil in medium saucepan or skillet. Sauté onions until tender and lightly browned. Mix mushrooms with mashed potatoes. Season to taste with salt and pepper.

Mushroom Filling

2 cups mushrooms, finely chopped
1 onion, finely chopped
2 tablespoons oil, divided
Salt and freshly ground black pepper

Heat 1 tablespoon oil in medium skillet. Add onion and sauté until tender and lightly browned. Remove onions with slotted spoon, set aside, and add remaining oil to pan. Add mushrooms and sauté, stirring, until tender. Combine mushrooms and onions and season to taste with salt and pepper.

To Assemble Knishes:

Preheat oven to 400° F.
Lightly flour rolling pin and work surface. Roll out dough, making a thin sheet, about 1/8" thick. Use a cookie cutter to make 3" rounds. Place a heaping teaspoon of filling on each round. Moisten half of the outer edge of each round with a pastry brush or finger dipped in a little water. Fold rounds over in half-moon shapes. Prick tops with fork. Bake on greased cookie sheet for 20 minutes or until golden brown. Watch carefully for the last few minutes to make sure they don't burn. Makes about 24 small knishes.

Tip: Use instead of matzoh balls in Golden Glow Soup

Moc Chopped Liver

A great dish for those who will eat lentils, healthy and delicious, and can be prepared the day before.

1/2 package brown lentils (1/2 pound)
1 large diced onion
1 cup chopped walnuts
Salt to taste

Put lentils in a 2 or 3 quart pot, and cover with water. Use water sparingly so that lentils absorb all the water. More water can be added as needed. Bring water to a boil, partially cover and simmer for about 45 minutes. Check to make sure water has not boiled off, and add water as needed.

Sauté onions until lightly golden and tender.
Put lentils, walnuts and onions in food processor, purée until slightly coarse.
Salt to taste. Chill about 2 hours. Serve with matzoh rounds or on lettuce leaves.

Cauliflower, Onions and Lemon

This recipe is from Sara Feldman, who designed the cover of this cookbook, and whose work has beautified several of our other books. It's a quick dish to be made in a microwave, a palatable side dish to a heavy meal.

1 medium cauliflower
1 large onion
1 lemon
1/4 cup water

Clean cauliflower and break into flowerets
Put water in bottom of round microwave dish with cover
Place onions on bottom of dish
Place cauliflower flowerets over onion
Squeeze lemon well over all
Cover dish. Microwave 5-6 minutes
Serves 5-6

Artichokes in Lemon Sauce

Another light vegetable dish that is especially welcome with a heavy meal.

6 artichokes, fresh or canned
grated rind from 2 lemons
2 quarts cold water
1 defrosted, drained 12 ounce bag of frozen mixed vegetables (peas and carrots)

Fill a 2 quart saucepan with water, put lemon rinds in the water, and set aside. Peel and clean the outer leaves of the artichokes. Core out the centers. Put stems into the acidulated water with the artichoke hearts, to prevent them from turning black.

Sauce:

Juice of two lemons
2 teaspoons of sugar
1/4 cup olive oil
2 cups water
Salt and pepper to taste
Chopped fresh dill (optional)

Put all ingredients into a saucepan and bring to a roiling boil, turn heat to low. Place artichokes with hearts down in the middle of the pot. Arrange drained, mixed vegetables around artichokes. Sprinkle salt, pepper and dill. Cover, simmer gently for about 30 minutes, or until artichokes are tender.
Do not overcook, or artichokes will get mushy.

> Why is this night different from all other nights?
> Because on this night, we dip our vegetables twice.
> Artichoke leaves make for great dipping.

Spiced Chickpeas and Rice

For those who eat rice and legumes, this dish can be served as an accompanying vegetable dish, or as a main dish.

1 cup uncooked chickpeas,
3 cups water
1 tablespoon oil
1 large onion, minced
1 large green pepper, diced
1 large tomato, cubed
1/2 teaspoon salt
1 1/2 teaspoons cumin, or to taste
1 8 ounce can of tomato sauce
1 cup brown rice (optional)
2 cups water for rice

The night before, soak chickpeas in water. In the morning, bring water to boil, and let simmer 3-4 hours in large pot partially covered. Test for done. Chickpeas should be soft but not mushy. Do not overcook, or they will fall apart.

Cook brown rice in water.
While rice is cooking, sauté onion in small amount of oil in large skillet. When oil is absorbed, add small amounts of water until onion is translucent and tender. Add green pepper, cook 5 minutes. Add tomato, cook another 5 minutes. Add tomato sauce. Drain chickpeas and add to skillet. Add salt and cumin, cover and simmer for about five minutes.
Optional: Serve over rice.
Serves 6-8.

Variations: Dish can be varied according to taste, with red pepper instead of green pepper, or by substituting a tablespoon of chili powder for the cumin, for those who like a spicier dish.

Eggplant Caviar

The next two dishes are good standbys and make great spreads on matzoh

2 medium size eggplants
1 medium size onion, chopped
2 tablespoons oil
1 tablespoon minced parsley
salt and pepper to taste
1 tablespoon fresh lemon juice, or to taste

Preheat Oven 350 F
Cut eggplants in half, lengthwise, bake 15-20 minutes until fork can pierce eggplant easily. Scoop the flesh out of the skin, mash, and mix with remaining ingredients. Serve in a bowl, surrounded by matzoh squares, or on lettuce leaves.

Guacamole

The secret to good guacamole is to use ripe (but not over-ripe) avocadoes. The dish needs almost nothing else.

2 ripe avocadoes
1 garlic clove, minced
1 tablespoon onion minced
1 tablespoon fresh lemon juice
salt to taste

Purée avocadoes in food processor. Mix in other ingredients. Serve as a spread on matzoh crackers.
Serves 6-8

Tip: Vary amount of lemon juice, garlic, salt, or onion according to taste. Some like their guacamole hot, others like it tame. Suit yourself.

Oriental Cabbage and Green Apple Slaw

1/2 large head green cabbage, or 1 whole small cabbage
1 large granny smith apple
2-3 ribs of celery, diced
2-3 tablespoons sesame oil, to taste
dash of mild vinegar

Shred cabbage in food processor
Shred apple, but not too fine
Mix cabbage and apple; add diced celery
Mix in oil and vinegar
Adjust taste to preference with salt

Variation: Add 1 tablespoon diced parsley or cilantro
Add 1/2 cup chopped walnuts

Baked Red Onions In Brown Rice Syrup

This is an exceptionally easy dish to make and looks beautiful

5-6 small red onions,
10 tablespoons brown rice syrup or honey
1/2 cup water

Preheat oven to 350 F.
Peel and cut in half each red onion
Scoop a little hole in the center of each half onion and fill with 1/2 tablespoon brown rice syrup or honey. Place all the halves in a casserole dish large enough to hold them, pour in water on bottom of casserole, cover and bake 1/2 hour. Serves ten.

Variation: Add slices of 2 granny smith apples around bottom and sides of baking dish.

Vegetable and Fruit Kugel

A variation on a dish in the Pesach Cookbook edited by the Beth Pinchas Sisterhood in Brookline, MA. But it is an old favorite and can't be omitted. The next three dishes derive from the same source

1 cup grated carrots
1 cup grated granny smith apples
1 cup grated potatoes
1 cup raisins
1/2 cup matzoh meal
1/2 teaspoon cinnamon
1/2 teaspoon salt
1/4 cup plus 1 tablespoon oil
2 tablespoons lemon juice

Preheat oven to 350 F
Combine all the ingredients.
Spread into two small ungreased loaf pans. Bake 45 minutes. Let cool for 10 minutes
Serves 8

Variation: sprinkle 1/2 cup ground walnuts mixed with cinnamon over each loaf 10 minutes before taking out of oven.

Sweet Potato Nut Balls

1 1/2 cups mashed sweet potatoes
1/4 cup orange juice
2 tablespoons sugar
chopped pecans

Preheat oven to 350 F
Peel sweet potatoes, cut in chunks and cook until tender enough to mash.
Mix in orange juice and sugar with mashed sweet potatoes
Shape mixture into 12 balls, using approximately 2 tablespoons for each ball.
Roll the balls in chopped pecans
Place on lightly greased cookie sheet
Bake 15 minutes. Yields 12 balls

Sweet Potato Orange Pudding

Use organic sweet potatoes for all recipes that call for this vegetable. It's worth the extra money. Choose sweet potatoes that are medium in size and not wrinkled or old looking. It makes a difference in the taste.

1 1/2 cups grated raw sweet potatoes
3/4 cup water
1/4 cup sugar
3/4 cup orange juice
1/2 teaspoon salt
1/4 teaspoon cinnamon
1/8 teaspoon ground cloves
1/2 stick melted margarine
grated rind of 1/2 orange

Preheat oven to 350F
Blend sweet potatoes with water, sugar, orange juice, salt and spices.
Stir in melted margarine and orange rind.
Pour into greased small loaf pan. Cover with aluminum foil.
Bake 30 minutes. Uncover, bake 30 minutes longer or until knife inserted in center comes out clean.
Serves 6. (Can be doubled and baked in 2 loaf pans.)

Split Pea Spread

1 cup split peas
3 1/4 cups water
1 grated carrot
1 small onion, chopped
2 ribs celery, diced finely
1 teaspoon celery salt
salt and pepper to taste

Bring split peas to a rapid boil in water
Add carrots and celery, onions and spices
Boil 15 minutes
Remove from heat, blend thoroughly, refrigerate.
Serve as a spread with matzoh squares or rounds

Stuffed Kishke

An old time favorite adapted to a non-meat recipe, and tastier.

8 ounces matzoh meal (about 1 3/4 cups)
1 medium onion, grated fine
1 large carrot, grated fine
3/4 teaspoon salt, or to taste
1/4 teaspoon pepper, or to taste
1 large celery rib, grated fine
4 tablespoons melted margarine

Preheat oven to 350^0 F.
Mix ingredients together and shape into 2 long rolls, each about 2 " in diameter.
Grease 2 pieces of foil; place rolls on foil and wrap tightly, but don't squeeze.
Place rolls on baking sheet.
Bake 1 hour.
Open foil and bake another 15 minutes, to brown.
Cool slightly before slicing.

Tip: May be made in advance and served cold.
To reheat, lightly cover rolls with foil and place in oven for about 10 minutes.
Can be reheated in microwave. Cut into 2" pieces.
Serves 8. Recipe can be doubled.

Beet Salad

Beets are a nuisance to clean because their color runs, but they are very nutritious and when cooked, add a wonderful color to a meal.

2 beets, grated
1/2 head cabbage, shredded
3 carrots, grated,
1 apple, diced
1/4 cup lemon juice
1/2 cup oil
handful of raisins

Toss all ingredients into a bowl, mix well, chill

Variations: Add sunflower seeds, chopped walnuts, crushed pineapple or other fruit

Roasted Beets

6-8 beets cut into chunks
1/2 cup olive oil
2-3 tablespoons crushed thyme

Preheat oven to 375 F
Lightly oil a large baking dish.
Mix dried thyme into olive oil.
Brush beet chunks with mixture and place in oiled baking dish.
Bake approximately 30-40 minutes
Serves 6-8

Herbed Matzoh Farfel

A handy ingredient during Pesach, it can add a piquant touch to many recipes, and is good for snacking. To 1 cup of matzoh farfel, add 2 tablespoons (or to taste) of your favorite herbs or spices, spread on oiled cookie sheet, toast in oven 3 minutes. If recipe calls for toasting, omit last step. If you do not have matzoh farfel you can grind matzohs in a food processor to farfel size.

Broiled Tomato Slices

4 medium size tomatoes, sliced 1/4 inch thick
1/4 cup olive oil
1 cup herbed matzoh farfel

Preheat oven 400 F
Place sliced tomatoes on oiled cookie sheet
Liberally sprinkle each slice with herbed matzoh farfel
Broil in oven 5 minutes
Serves 8-10

Stuffed Portobello Mushrooms

6 portobello mushrooms
1 cup herbed matzoh farfel
marinate sauce (optional)
(see potato-mushroom kugel, p. 47 for marinate recipe)

Preheat oven 400 F
Scrub portobello mushrooms with a soft brush to clean. Remove stems. Roast on oiled cookie sheet 20 minutes with or without marinating. Remove from oven. Sprinkle each mushroom with 1 tablespoon of herbed matzoh. Return to oven for 3-5 minutes
Serves 6

Variation: For an impressive presentation, combine the last two recipes. Place a tomato on each mushroom, sprinkle herbed matzoh farfel on tomato slices and return to oven for 3-5 minutes.

Wilted Kale with Pine Nuts and Raisins

1 to 1 1/2 pounds of kale
1/4 cup olive oil
1 cup pignoli nuts
1/2 cup or a large handful of raisins

Heat oil in very large skillet
Wash and shred kale into bite size pieces. Discard stems
Put washed kale into skillet and cook on low heat until kale is limp. Mix occasionally to keep kale from sticking to the skillet. Five minutes before kale is done, add pignoli nuts and raisins and stir to make sure all ingredients are coated with oil and cooked. Cool five minutes and serve
Serves 6-8

Tip: To reduce oil, oil skillet lightly, add shredded kale; after five minutes add half a cup of water, cover skillet, turn up heat until water boils, reduce immediately. Steam covered for about five minutes more.

Sweet and Sour Red Cabbage

From *The Jewish Vegetarian Year Cookbook,* this recipe is good for a large seder

4 pounds of red cabbage
1/3 cup vegetable oil
1 apple, preferably Granny Smith, peeled and diced
1/3 cup vinegar
1/2 cup currant jelly mixed with 1/2 cup water
1 1/2 teaspoons salt
1/4 cup sugar

Discard any tough outer leaves, and shred cabbage fine. Warm the oil in a large, heavy pot. Add the cabbage and apple. Cover and cook 5 minutes, shaking the pan frequently. Add the vinegar, currant jelly mixed with water, salt and sugar. Stir to combine thoroughly. Cook, covered, over low heat for 2 hours, stirring frequently and adding a little water if necessary. Taste and adjust the balance of sweet and sour to your liking.
Serves 8-12.

The Classic Tossed Salad

Everyone has their favorite ingredients, favorite salad dressing and favorite way of making the tossed salad. Following are recommendations. The balance of ingredients is up to you.

Miyoko Nishimoto in her book, *The Now and Zen Epicure,* has some sound advice about how to treat lettuce---the main ingredient in a tossed salad. "Whatever you do, the greens must be crisp." She states that you can bring back to life old or tired looking greens by soaking them in a bowl of cold water for fifteen minutes. "Drain or pat each leaf gently with a cloth or paper towels until dry; or use a salad spinner"(I prefer the salad spinner), and suggests that you do this even for fresh greens. Wrap greens in a moist towel or several layers of paper towels (if you've used towels to dry the lettuce leaves you can re-use them here) and then store lettuce in a plastic bag in the refrigerator. This should keep your lettuce crisp for weeks and save you the time of having to wash and dry them on the same evening you serve them. If you do wash your greens on the same day, do it a few hours in advance, spin dry, then let them sit in the spin dryer for a few hours until water droplets drain off the leaves. Next to wilted lettuce, the next worst sin is a wet salad.

Always tear lettuce leaves with your hands (don't cut them) into bite sizes. All the ingredients you put in a toss salad should, if possible, be bite size. Use only enough dressing to coat the salad; never over-use dressing. It's nice to use a variety of greens or lettuces, but don't use iceberg lettuce, unless you're in love with it. Of all the lettuces it has minimum nutritional value. As for the rest of the ingredients, here's a list you can choose from:

broccoli (lightly steamed), tomatoes, parsley, cilantro, cucumbers, grated carrots, steamed and chilled green beans, baked and chilled eggplant slices cut into bite size pieces, roasted and chilled red pepper slices, avocados, pitted olives

Use a good olive oil and a light vinegar, perhaps rice vinegar. If you like a more astringent taste in your salad, use balsamic vinegar. First toss the salad with the oil, then add your favorite herbs, then mix again thoroughly, then add vinegar and mix once more. My favorite salad mixture includes slices of avocado in the salad because it makes the salad creamy. Small cherry tomatoes and/or thinly sliced red onion or red cabbage add nice color. Small white beans, if you happen to have some left over, go well in salads. I also sometimes toss in roasted, cold eggplant chunks or roasted, cold portobello chunks.

Desserts

In the United States, we place too much emphasis on dessert and too often end a heavy meal with a rich, heavy dessert. By the time we reach dessert, our stomachs are in rebellion and our guests are groaning. In many European countries, dessert is fruit. And traditionally fruit has become the dessert of choice for many Pesach meals because it is difficult to bake cakes without leaven and the choice of baked goods is often limited. Traditional-- pre-vegetarian days, pre-health-conscious days—Pesach cakes were often made with nine and twelve eggs, perhaps to compensate for the lack of leaven. We were lucky to survive the dessert.

But great creations of fruit compotes , baked fruits and fresh fruit dishes were also created, and a vegetarian Pesach meal takes up this tradition. We emphasize fruit dishes, though there are chocolate covered cakes and sweet candies for those with a sweet tooth, and pies using matzo mixed with nuts and/or cinnamon for crusts.

For those who want to experiment further, Joan Nathan states in *The Jewish Holiday Kitchen* that "...baking soda, a pure product and not a leavening agent, can be used at Passover." She also gives the following equivalents for flour:

1 cup regular flour = 1/4 cup matzoh cake meal
= 3/4 cup potato starch

1/2 cup regular flour = 2 tablespoons matzoh cake meal
= 6 tablespoons potato starch

B'tay-avon

No Bake Chocolate Matzoh Roll

This was a longtime favorite in Israel when not every home had an oven in the early decades of the country, but the dessert has become popular here for obvious reasons. This recipe and the next two were featured in *The Jewish Vegetarian Year Cookbook.*

4 squares plain matzoh
Water for moistening matzoh
1/4 cup sugar
3 tablespoons strong coffee
4 oz. semi-sweet chocolate
1 tablespoon brandy(optional)
1 cup margarine at room temperature
3/4 cup chopped walnuts

Glaze:

2 ounces semi-sweet chocolate
3 tablespoons water

Garnish:

1 pint strawberries, washed but not hulled

In a large bowl, soak matzoh in water briefly. Drain water and crumble matzoh. Melt chocolate with coffee and sugar in the top of a double boiler or in a small bowl in a microwave oven. Add brandy, if using. Cool.

In a large mixing bowl, beat margarine until fluffy. Add chocolate mixture, beating well. Stir in matzoh and nuts.

Place a piece of wax paper about 2 feet long on a work surface. Use a large spoon to shape a mass about 10" long and 2" in diameter. Wrap the wax paper around it and shape it into a cylinder. Tuck the ends under, place on a plate, and refrigerate at least 3 hours until firm.

Melt glaze ingredients. Unwrap the roll, spoon glaze over it evenly, and chill again. To serve, arrange on platter surrounded by berries. Or serve slices on individual plates with some berries on the side. Slice with serrated knife. Serves 10-12. This dessert is very rich, so servings are small.

Elegant Curried Fruit

A versatile dish that can be served as a dessert if made with crust, or as an accompaniment to entrée if made without crust, or as a dessert by itself without the crust, or as a layered pie cake (see Variations)

Matzoh Farfel Pie Crust:

Melt 1/2 pound margarine, mix with 1/2 cup brown sugar.
Mix into 3 cups matzoh farfel to make a pie layer or crust. Press into a 9" pie plate and bake for about 20 minutes at 350^0 F.

Filling

1 large can of sliced peaches, drained
2 small cans of mandarin oranges, drained
1 teaspoon curry powder
Candied fruits (optional)

Drain canned fruit thoroughly. (Reserve fruit juices for later use if desired.) Arrange fruit on farfel crust. Sprinkle curry on top. Dot with candied fruits.

Curried fruit pie can be served warm or cold. If served warm, bake matzo farfel crust for only 15 minutes.

Variations: Eliminate curry and top with a sweet sauce.

Make 2 or 3 matzoh farfel crusts for a layered cake. Put peaches on first layer, cover with second crust, put apricots on second layer; cover with third crust. End with crust or with a layer of other fruit.

Curried fruit, without crust, can be served as a fruit dish to accompany entrée or as a "crustless" dessert with or without sauce on top.

Tip: It is important to drain and dry canned fruits thoroughly, or dessert will be runny and the crust will soften.

Prune Treats

A delicious confection for holiday nibbling.

2 pounds prunes, pitted, rinsed and drained
walnuts or pecan halves
1 cup sugar
2 cups sweet kiddush wine

Stuff each prune with a nut half.
Boil sugar and wine until sugar dissolves. Add prunes, simmer gently about 15 minutes. Refrigerate in covered container. Drain before serving. Recipe makes a lot and can be halved.

Tip: Serve with a sauce to dip prunes into.

Carrot Candy

Another favorite for nibbling. This one comes from Rose Friedman's *Jewish Vegetarian Cooking*. One of the earliest Jewish vegetarian cookbooks, it was published in England by the Jewish International Vegetarian Society. This treat is also commonly known as ingerblach.

1-1/2 pounds carrots, scraped and cleaned
2 cups (1 pound) sugar
3/4 cups orange juice
1/2 teaspoon ground cinnamon
1-1/2 teaspoon ground ginger
1 cupful ground or chopped nuts

Dice and boil carrots in a little water until tender. Drain and mash well.
Mix the sugar, orange juice, cinnamon and ginger into the carrots and cook on a very low heat for 20 minutes. Stir often to prevent sticking.
Add chopped nuts, and cook another 10 minutes. Remove from heat. Mixture should be thick.
Dampen a pastry board and spread mixture on it to a thickness of about 1/2 inch. Let cool. When cold, cut into squares and sprinkle with sugar.

Layered Matzoh Pudding

This dessert is also adapted from Rose Friedman's *Jewish Vegetarian Cooking*. Heat oven to 350 degrees

4-5 eating apples
4 matzohs
1/2 cup raisins, soaked briefly in hot water
1/4 cup margarine
2 tablespoons sugar
2 cups water
pinch sea salt
1 teaspoon ground cinnamon
3 tablespoons chopped nuts

Grate apples, or slice thinly. Dip matzohs in water to moisten, but not soften. Place one matzoh in bottom of greased pie dish.
Place a layer of grated apples on top of the matzo and sprinkle with raisins. Dot with margarine. Bake 15 minutes, or until lightly browned.
Serves 6
Variations: Moisten matzo in apple or orange juice for a different taste sensation and/or sprinkle confectionery sugar and/or ginger lightly on top.

Rice Pudding

A delectable and versatile dessert when you have many guests for dinner.

1 1/2 cups short grain, sweet white rice
3 1/4 cups water
1 small can of coconut milk
1 tablespoon cinnamon
1 cup of white raisins
1 cup chopped walnuts

Cook rice in water 45 minutes until water is absorbed. Soak raisins in hot water five minutes. Mix coconut milk, cinnamon and raisins into the rice. Top with walnuts.
Serves 10-12
Variations: 1 cup of orange juice instead of coconut milk. Top with sliced apricots, dried or fresh, sliced pitted sour cherries, vary according to taste.

Six Ways of Looking At A Baked Apple

Baked apples are one of my favorite desserts because you can vary them according to your taste and imagination. Following are some suggestions. This dessert is also nice because you can make early in the day.

6 apples
1 to 1 1/2 cup water
2 tablespoons cinnamon

Preheat oven 350 F
Wash, core apples, score skin from core half way down. Place apples in a casserole with a cover. Sprinkle cinnamon into each core and on the bottom of casserole and pour the water over the apples and on the bottom of the casserole. Bake 25 minutes uncovered. Cover and continue baking for the next ten minutes. Test with a fork. If apples aren't done, bake a few more minutes, until apples are still firm but soft enough for a fork to penetrate.

Variations: They are infinite. Place a tablespoon of chopped walnuts into each apple core five minutes before apples are done baking, or after apples are removed from the oven.
Replace water with wine
Mix 1 tablespoon of vanilla flavoring into water
Squeeze a lemon or lime on to the apples and bake squeezed skins with the apples . Garnish with lemons or limes thinly sliced and placed into sliced openings of the apples.
Top with chocolate skillet sauce or orange sauce (see recipes, p. 69) and/or chopped walnuts.

Chocolate Bananas

A treat for children and the young in heart

6 ounces semi-sweet chocolate
3 tablespoons margarine
6 bananas or four oranges peeled and sliced 1/2 inch slices

Melt chocolate in double boiler. Add margarine and stir until blended. Remove from heat. Cut bananas in half and cover with chocolate. Decorate with pitted grapes.

Compotes

Like baked apples, there are many varieties of compotes, and they are traditional for Pesach. The following recipe is somewhat unusual and was featured in *The Jewish Vegetarian Year Cookbook.*

Strawberry-Rhubarb Compote

2 cups 3/4 inch rhubarb slices (about 10 ounces)
2 medium apples, peeled, cored, finely diced
1/3-1/2 cup sugar
1/2-3/4 cup water
1 quart strawberries, hulled and halved

In a heavy-bottomed 3 quart saucepan, combine rhubarb, apple, 1/3 cup sugar, and enough water to cover. Bring to a boil. Lower heat and simmer about 10 minutes. Stir occasionally. When fruit is tender, mash apples and rhubarb into a sauce. Add berries , stir 5 minutes over low heat. Taste, add sugar as desired. Serve warm or cold.
Serves 8
Tip: Can be served as a topping over cake

Spiced Citrus Compote

An unusual and refreshing compote from the Beth Pinchas Sisterhood.

6 large oranges
1/2 cup sugar
10 whole cloves
1/4 teaspoon salt
2 medium grapefruit
2 tablespoons lemon juice
1 teaspoon cinnamon

Grate orange peel for 1 tablespoon of peel. Set aside. Peel and section oranges and grapefruit into a bowl. In a quart saucepan, over medium heat, cook sugar, lemon juice, salt, cloves, cinnamon and 1 cup water for 10 minutes, or until mixture becomes a light syrup and volume is reduced in half. Pour syrup over fruit, stir in orange peel. Remove cloves, cover and chill in refrigerator.

Sherbert and Sauces

The following are adapted from the *Beth Pinchas Pesach Cookbook,* and are great desserts when children are around.

3 bananas
3 cups sugar
3 cups water
juice of 3 oranges
juice of 3 lemons

Beat bananas until creamy. Add remaining ingredients. Mix well. Pour into refrigerator tray. Stir every 20 minutes until mixture is "mushy." Then freeze. Serves 4-6

Orange Sauce

1/3 cup sugar
1/4 teaspoon salt
1/2 teaspoon grated orange rind
1 tablespoon potato starch
1 cup orange juice

Blend sugar, starch and salt in a saucepan. Add rind. Stir juice into mixture gradually. Cook over low heat stirring constantly until mixture thickens. Makes 1 to 1 1/2 cups sauce. Use as topping for a dessert.

Skillet Sauce

1 cup coarsely chopped walnuts
1 cup semi-sweet chocolate pieces
1/4 cup margarine

Melt margarine in a heavy skillet. Add walnuts. Stir over moderate heat until margarine is lightly browned. Remove from heat. Add chocolate pieces and stir until mixture is melted and smooth.
Makes 1 1/4 cups. Use as topping for dessert

Tip: Use as topping for sherbert for an extra rich dessert. The combination of chocolate and citrus fruit is wonderful.

Index for Recipes

Other Books in the JAR Series from Micah Publications.
For full list of Micah titles reviews and buying information, see our website,
www.micahbooks.com

General:

Vegetarian Judaism--A Guide for Everyone. Roberta Kalechofsky, Ph.D. Foreword by Rabbi David Rosen. Examines the problem of meat from a Jewish perspective and promotes the values of eco-kashrut. $15.95

Judaism and Animal Rights: Classical and Contemporary Responses. ed. Roberta Kalechofsky. Forty-one articles by rabbis, scholars, physicians, and historians on subjects of shechitah, vegetarianism, and animal research. $17.95

Rabbis and Vegetarianism: An Evolving Tradition. ed. Roberta Kalechofsky. Seventeen essays by Orthodox, Conservative, Reform and Reconstructionist rabbis on vegetarianism. $10.00

The Jewish Vegetarian Perpetual book of Days: Combines Jewish vegetarian thought with your personal diary of events. Includes a ten year Jewish calendar. $15.00

Cookbooks

The Jewish Vegetarian Year Cookbook, Kalechofsky and Rasiel. Recipes and menus for all the major Jewish holidays. Includes a Tu b'Shvat haggadah. $16.95

For Pesach

Haggadah For the Liberated Lamb: For a seder that celebrates compassion for all creatures. Bilingual, egalitarian, vegetarian, traditional, illustrated. 162 pgs. Paperback edition: $14.95

Cloth edition: $24.95

Haggadah For the Vegetarian Family. Bilingual, egalitarian, traditional, illustrated, 72 pgs. Appropriate for inter-generational seder. $10.00

Journey of the Liberated Lamb: Reflections on a Vegetarian Seder. Roberta Kalechofsky. History of Jewish worship told as a story for children. Teaches about continuity and change in Jewish worship. Suggestions for projects for children. Historic notes for adults. Pamphlet. $6.00

For Children

A Boy, A Chicken and the Lion of Judah---How Ari Became a Vegetarian. Roberta Kalechofsky. Winner of the 1996 "Kind Writers Make Kind Readers" Award from the Fund for Animals. "Giving this to your child...is a promise...to understand. *The Jerusalem Report.* $8.00

My Time: A Do-It-Yourself, Color-Me-In-Jewish Humane Calendar. Teaches children about Jewish time and its relationship to nature, as well as the Jewish tradition concerning animals. $5.00

The Green Mitzvah Booklets. Richard Schwartz and Roberta Kalechofsky. Excellent for educators and students. Covers subjects such as vegetarianism and concern for animals in individual booklets. Individually priced. $15.00 for the set of four.